Where's the Wheat?

Food Storage Your Family Will Eat

By

Juli Brown

This book is a work of fiction. Places, events, and situations in this story are purely fictional. Any resemblance to actual persons, living or dead, is coincidental.

ISBN: 1-4107-2776-9 (e-book)
ISBN: 1-4107-2777-7 (Paperback)

This book is printed on acid free paper.

1stBooks - rev. 03/29/03

Dedication

For my family.
They always kept their sense of humor, no matter what I served for dinner.

Beginning a Food Storage Program

So often food storage brings to mind visions of wheat filled buckets. But what if your family doesn't like to eat wheat? Times of financial difficulty are stressful enough without trying to get your family to eat food they don't like. The concept is to store what you like and eat what you store. If your family likes freshly baked whole wheat bread, then store what you need to continue to provide that. If your family is more likely to eat white bread, then store white flour. A familiar and varied diet is possible to achieve from food storage. Most of the foods that we eat on a daily basis can be stored for a year or more.

Food storage is not a new concept. We have been told for years to gather and store the things we would need to survive for a year. This seems like an overwhelming task. We have so many things to do just to get through the day, that the thought of planning and obtaining a year of food and supplies feels impossible. Broken down into steps and goals, this daunting project can be accomplished. Whether you are planning for one person or a large family, keep in mind what your family's needs are. Tailor everything around those wants and needs and you will be successful. We don't always know if or when we will ever need our food storage. However, great peace of mind comes from careful planning.

One day my husband came home from work and announced that the company he worked for was moving overseas. The entire company was shutting down operations here in our area and he would soon be out of a job. We were a young family with small children. After some discussion and planning, we decided that this would be an ideal time for him to return to school to finish his degree. We had enough money in savings and food in storage. Our goal was to live off what we had for one year, without anyone else knowing what we were doing. We opted to not tell our friends or our family that we were out of work, and see if we could do this without help.

We were able to have family and friends over for dinner and take food to friends when a new baby was born or someone was ill. We were still able to feed our family well. At the end of the year, we announced what had been going on. Our extended family was quite surprised at how well everything had gone. Our family ate the same foods to which we were accustomed, and we never had to change our diet. We were able to take care of ourselves, which is the whole purpose of having a food storage. We personalized our food storage to include foods that our family enjoyed on a daily basis. This took planning and organizing, but it paid off.

Beginning a food storage program will require some thought. First decide what your current situation is. Do you have some food already set aside? Are you at the beginning stages of acquiring food storage? How much time and energy are you willing to put into storing food? The answers to all of these questions will determine what kind of food storage plan you will have.

Think about the people you are feeding on a daily basis. How many people do you feed? What are their ages? Will the number of people in your household be changing within the next year? Be sure to consider any special dietary needs of family members. Infants may require special foods, as do family members with medical needs. You may decide that you wish to include food in your storage plan that will allow you to take food to others when necessary, for example, the birth of a friend's baby or a funeral.

Plan for holiday celebrations, such as Christmas, Thanksgiving, birthdays, etc. These holidays will come around every year, so it is important to continue having traditional family foods for these celebrations. Having the ingredients on hand to make a birthday cake for a family party can make a stressful time seem so much easier to handle. It is nice to be able to provide your family's favorite holiday foods during family celebrations.

Remember to include medications, toiletries, first aid and hygiene supplies. Over the counter medications will last on the shelf for a year at a time, but be sure to check the expiration dates on all medications. Do not use these products after the expiration date. Medications can lose their effectiveness and are sensitive to light and heat. Always store them in a cabinet away from heat, light and moisture. Your favorite brands of shampoo, soap, lip moisturizer, and hygiene products are welcome additions to any storage. Buy these items when they are on sale and stock up on them. A few cents here and there saved on items will add up quickly.

Set goals for yourself regarding your food storage. Break this enormous task up into smaller, reachable goals. Perhaps you could begin by obtaining a two-week or a month supply instead of trying to buy for a whole year at once. Be aware that providing food for yourself or your family will take time, effort and dedication. Take inventory of the foods you have on hand right now. Consider how much room you have or are willing to create to store the food you gather. Decide whether you have more time or more money and plan to gather your food storage accordingly.

If you have more money than time, you can get someone else to put together your year supply. If, however, you decide that you have more time than money, realize that you are going to have to do the legwork yourself. You can recruit your family to help you. You may have better success at recruiting a friend or a relative to go shopping with you. That would make this less work, and more enjoyable. You never know though, it is always worth a try to get your husband and children to jump on the bandwagon. Make this a fun family activity. Clip coupons, look for hidden storage spaces or to plan your next food storage item. Family input is important. This will teach your children how to store food when they are adults, and helps them to feel like a participating member of the family. It also ensures that everyone gets a say in what food will be stored and eaten.

Relax, have some fun with this. It is going to be a lot of work, but you can choose whether the work is stressful or pleasant. You don't have to reach this goal in a day or a week. It will take time and patience. You might as well have fun in the process.

Types of Food Storage

Basic foods come to mind when thinking about food storage. It is good to start with the basic necessities. These are the foods that are needed to sustain life. Include foods such as flour, sugar, oil, yeast, milk and water. Basics are relatively inexpensive and are easy to obtain. Water is especially important to have stored. Without water it is difficult to cook or clean. You can add other basic foods to your storage, as you are able, such as oatmeal, rice, beans and dairy. Amounts you will need to store are listed in the next section.

Storing the basics provides for little variety. Appetite fatigue is the drawback to this type of plan. This will however sustain life, and can be done in a nutritionally balanced fashion. If you choose to store only the basics, learn to use them now. Incorporate these foods into your family's daily diet so that they are used to them before you have an opportunity to totally rely on this type of food. Now is the time to experiment with new recipes and new ways of cooking basic simple foods. If your family never eats wheat, and wheat is what you have stored, you may be in for some major adjustments if you ever need to live off of your food storage.

Another option is to store only dehydrated or pre-packaged food. While these are incredibly convenient they also need lots of water to cook them. If you choose to store these foods, remember to compensate by adding extra water to your storage. Pre-packaged or dehydrated foods may not get eaten on a daily basis making them hard to rotate as often as needed. Also, these foods are expensive. If you are trying to do this on a tight budget, it might be better to limit the amounts of these that you store. Prepackaged and dehydrated foods come in a wide variety making appetite fatigue less likely. They taste good and are easy to prepare. During times of stress it is convenient to be able to just open a package, add water and cook foods that are familiar. Some types of prepackaged complete meals are available at grocery stores and food warehouses.

Storing foods that you eat on a daily basis now will give you many benefits. This will provide you with a wide variety of choices, further reducing the chance of appetite fatigue. Your family will be familiar with the foods and will be more likely to eat them. Comfort foods can help ease stress in times of trial. You will also already know how to prepare the food. You can store just the ingredients you need to cook from scratch or you can prepare your own convenience foods. By storing foods that you use daily now, you will be able to rotate the food easily and conveniently. They are easy to obtain where you usually shop for groceries. The foods you serve your family daily also go on sale and can be purchased using coupons. This will reduce your costs and allow you to purchase more food with the amount of money you have budgeted.

How Much Do I Need?

You can choose to buy the basic necessities and get these stored before you start with a menu plan. The advantage to this is that the basics are relatively inexpensive and easily attainable. These foods are nutritious and will sustain life. It is better to have a year supply of the basics than no food storage at all. Additional foods may be added later for variety and comfort.

How much you will need to store depends on several things. How many people are in your family? What are their ages? Keep in mind special dietary needs of infants and those with medical conditions. Also consider whether or not the number of people in your family will be changing within the next year. Do you need to plan for a new baby, or are you gaining a son or daughter in law? Remember, young couples just starting out probably won't begin their married life with adequate food storage. Plan to include them when deciding how much you need to store. When close members of our family get married, we give them a start on their food storage as a gift. This gives them a sense of security and helps with the financial burden of gathering a year supply.

Make a list of the number of people in your family. Next list the foods you plan to store and the amount needed per person. Multiply the amount by the number of people to get your total needed.

Let's start with water. You will need a minimum of 14 gallons per person for a two-week supply. This will give you the bare amount for drinking and hygiene. If at all possible, double this amount. Empty, clean two-liter soda bottles can be used to store water in the house. These are small enough to handle, yet hold enough for a person to drink for a day. If you plan to store dehydrated foods, adjust the amount you store accordingly. If you have infants, small children or family members with special needs, you will need more water for hygiene. Include water to mix formula for the baby. Rotate the water at least once a year so that the flavor remains palatable. Include some water for your garden if you don't live in an area that receives enough natural rainfall.

We discovered the need for extra water the hard way. Our main water line to the house broke. The only way to repair it was to dig up the yard down to the pipe, take out the damaged one and replace it. To do this we had to turn off all the water to the house. This left no time to fill up the bathtubs with any emergency water. Two of our family members were ill. One of them was on life support. This required extra water to clean equipment and to bathe the child that was sick. We went through what we thought was a two week supply of water in one weekend. Fortunately we had access to more water from a neighbor's hose and from the grocery store. The valuable lesson that we learned was to actually try completely living off of what we stored. Had we done so, we would have known how much water we needed for our family's specific needs. Remember, all the amounts listed are guidelines. Your family may need more or less than what is listed here.

Another important part of the basic food storage is grain. Grains can include wheat, flour, oatmeal and rice. Each adult will need 300-400 pounds per year. Store enough wheat or flour to bake bread and tortillas. Oatmeal and rice will help to add some variety to your diet. Remember to include yeast. Rotate the yeast to keep it fresh.

Beans come in many different types and flavors. These add some variety to your diet as well as much needed nutrition. Beans can be dried or canned. You will need 34 pounds per adult. Vary the type of beans you store so that you reduce appetite fatigue as much as possible. Pork and beans can be used as a side dish or a main dish. Ranch style beans can be used to make chili. Refried beans can be made into burritos or tostadas. Although it isn't a bean, peanut butter is a familiar food and one that most children are willing to eat. It will serve the same purpose as beans. Beans are not a complete protein by themselves. They can be added to cheese to make a complete protein. Beans can also be added to homemade breads and cakes. This will increase the nutritional value of foods, without altering the flavor.

Dairy products will help you to be able to cook familiar foods. They will also add necessary proteins and vitamins for good nutrition. Milk can be stored as a powder, evaporated, or sweetened condensed. Powdered milk loses its flavor after about 2 years on the shelf. It will remain usable for several years after that however. Milk can also be stored in the form of hot chocolate. Sometimes children will find hot chocolate more palatable than powdered white milk. You will need 16 pounds of milk per adult. Another 10 pounds of dairy is also recommended. This can include butter or margarine, eggs and cheeses. Butter, margarine, eggs and cheese can be purchased as a powder and stored for long periods on the shelf. You can also store butter, margarine and cheese in the freezer for up to one year safely. Because these are foods that you use everyday, these are easy to rotate.

Salt, sugars, oils and fats will complete the basics. 5 pounds of salt, 50 pounds of sugar and 4 gallons of fats or oils per adult are needed. Sugars can include white, brown or powdered. Honey will also work as a sweetener. Fats and oils can include shortening, liquid oils, canned sprays, mayonnaise and salad dressings. Shortening also comes in a butter flavor that can be used in baking. Fats and oils must be rotated to ensure freshness. They have a shorter shelf life than some other foods, so be sure to check the use by dates on the labels.

Creating a Plan

To begin planning your food storage, you will need to fill out the menu forms. Think about the foods that your family likes to eat. Include snacks if they eat them also. Write down all the foods included in the meal. This will help you to make sure that the meals are nutritious and well balanced at a glance. This also helps to eliminate repetition. See the example menu pages included to give you an idea of how to fill out the menus. The sample menus are the ones that I use for my family. There are 5 blank menu forms included in this book. This will give you enough spaces to include a months worth of meals and extra spaces for Holiday and family celebration meals.

Use these blank forms to write down the meals that you normally fix for your own family. If you have 7 dinners that you rotate, then you will only need one blank menu form. Make four copies of the completed form to give you a month of meals. If you have 14 different meals, then use two forms, etc. Fill our as many forms as you need to complete a month of menus. If you are serving 14 meals, you will be writing down the same meals approximately twice a month. To plan for a year's worth of meals off of this list, you would serve that each of those meals 24 times. If you have 30 different meals that you serve your family, then you would serve each meal 12 times during the year. By serving as many different meals as possible, your family will be less likely to have appetite fatigue. Look at the sample menus for ideas on different meals that your family might enjoy. Included at the back of this booklet are recipes for some of the sample menus.

<u>Time to Shop</u>

Now it's time to go shopping. Using these menu sheets, write a grocery list. Include all the ingredients needed to prepare the meals on the menus. List all the amounts for the same foods on the same line and add up your totals. If I need 2 boxes of cereal for that week, and I plan to use that week's menu 12 times during the year, I will need 24 boxes of cereal to be able to serve that week's menu for one year.

Repeat this process for each of your weekly menus until you have completed a months worth of meals. Make a master shopping list for each of the weekly menus. If you typically do your grocery shopping once a month instead of weekly, make a master list for a month. The master list helps you to take advantage of sale items by knowing exactly how much you need. You can save time and money while purchasing in bulk without waste.

I have included a sample grocery list for one of the weekly menus that we use at our house. On the sample grocery list there are two amounts for each food listed. One is the amount I would need to buy for one week. The amount in parenthesis is the amount I would need to purchase for a year.

FOOD STORAGE
DAILY MENU RECORD

	Sunday	Monday	Tuesday	Wednesday	Thursday	Friday	Saturday
Breakfast	blueberry muffin	pumpkin bread	cream of wheat	strawberry muffins	banana bread	blueberry pancakes	cold cereal
	Milk	Milk	raisins	milk	milk	milk	toast
			Milk				milk
Lunch	bean w/bacon soup	Haystacks	turkey sandwich	fiesta soup	beef pot pie	chicken noodle soup	h.m. pizza
	cheese	tortilla chips	potato salad	crackers	apple chips	crackers	fruit whip
		beans, cheese		peanut butter		peanut butter cups	
	crackers	onions, chilies					
PM Snack	marshmallo w parfait	Chocolate peanut butter Dessert	pudding cones	gelatin fruit bouquet	rocky road pudding	peachy-orange ring	self layering-dessert
Supper	tacos	chicken pot pie	pepper steak	hamburger gravy	sweet n sour	sloppy joes	fajitas
	spanish rice	fruited tilt	rice	mashed potatoes	chicken	macaroni salad	tortilla
	mixed vegetables		biscuits	fruit sorbet	rice	fruit	steak strips
	pineapple		vegetables		fruit		chips, salsa
Evening Snack	pudding	apple cider	fruited marble	pudding pizza	jell-o jewel	boston crème pie	fruited chiffon-
	cookies	Dessert	dessert				squares

13

Sample Grocery List

2 boxes blueberry muffin mix (24)

1 box pumpkin bread mix (12)

1 box cream of wheat cereal (12)

1 box strawberry muffin mix (12)

1 box banana bread mix (12)

1 box cold cereal (12)

1 gallon milk (12)

2 cans bean with bacon soup (24)

1 can Fiesta soup (12)

2 cans chicken noodle soup (12)

12 ounce pkg American cheese (144 oz)

1 box soup crackers (12)

1 loaf sandwich bread (24 loaves)

8 ounces sliced turkey (96 oz)

1 can refried beans (12)

1 bag tortilla chips (12)

8 ounces cheddar cheese (96 oz)

1 can green chiles (12)

5 pound bag potatoes (60 lbs)

1 jar peanut butter (12)

3 cups apple chips (36 cups)

7 jars fruit (84)

1 Pizza crust (12)

1 jar pizza sauce (12)

4 ounces mozzarella cheese (48 oz)

1 bag marshmallows (12)

12 ounces chocolate chips (144 oz)

5 pound bag flour (60 lbs)

8 boxes of Jell-O (96)

7 boxes pudding (84)

1 box graham crackers (12)

1 white cake mix (12)

1 chocolate cake mix (12)

1 bottle vegetable oil (12)

1 pkg hamburger buns (12)

6 ounces macaroni pasta (72)

1 whole chicken (12)

2 lbs round steak (24 lbs)

3 lbs hamburger (36 lbs)

1 jar salsa (12)

1 bottle apple cider (12)

1 container whipped topping (12)

1 dozen eggs (12)

1 lb margarine (12)

2 cups white sugar (24)

2 cups brown sugar (24)

6 ice cream cones (72)

6 cups rice (72 cups)

6 cans assorted vegetables (72 cans)

8 cups biscuit mix (96 cups)

1 jar sweet and sour sauce (12)

I have found that making a menu sheet and a grocery list helps me to see at a glance how much food I need to buy. For instance, in my house I know I will need to have 200 pounds of hamburger to feed my family for a year. This was easy to figure out because I listed all the amounts of hamburger needed to make each meal during a week, a month, and a year, added them up, and entered my total on the grocery list. As you buy foods on this list keep track of the purchases so that you don't waste money on duplicate purchases. Keep this list with you each time you go to the store, along with the money that you have set aside for food storage.

When you see an advertised or unadvertised special, check you list and your money will be spent wisely. For example, I need 36 cans of green chilies for a year. When chilies go on sale at 3 cans for a dollar, I know how many to get without over or under buying. For $9.00 I can purchase a year supply of green chilies.

I have my grocery money separated into two categories. One category is for my monthly groceries and the other for food storage. Any money I save on monthly groceries also goes into food storage.

You will notice as you make your list that foods begin to fall into categories, such as meats, breads, dairy etc. Once you list is made, it might be a good idea for you to organize the list by where the items are located in the grocery store. This will make shopping easier. Several stores in my area have store layout maps available at the customer service desk.

Rotating Inventory

Now that you have used your master shopping lists to purchase your food, you will want to make sure that you use and rotate the food. The easiest way to keep track of what you have used from the pantry is to keep track of which foods you have served your family during the week or the month.

After you have made your menus and grocery lists, make menu cards using 3x5 or 4x6 cards. Write on each card the name of the meal and all the ingredients needed to make the meal. For example, if you are serving chicken and rice casserole, green beans, applesauce, biscuits and milk for dinner, write at the top of the card: "Chicken and Rice". See below for an example.

Chicken and Rice

8 oz cooked diced chicken

2 cups rice

1 can cream of chicken soup

¼ cup onions (dehydrated or fresh)

1 can green beans

1 jar applesauce

6 servings margarine

6 servings honey

2 cups biscuit mix

½ cup milk

4 servings milk

If you are planning to serve this meal once a month, you will need to buy enough ingredients to serve this meal 12 times. If you plan to serve this meal twice a month, then buy enough ingredients to serve it 24 times in a year. Make one menu card for each time you serve a meal. For example, if you serve the chicken and rice meal twice in one month, make two menu cards for it.

Put all your menu cards into a file box. When you serve a meal, remove the card, and place it in the back of the box behind a divider. When it is time to make your shopping list, remove the used cards from the file, copy the ingredients that you have used from the cards onto your shopping list. This will help you to keep track of what has been used from your food storage, making your inventory automatic. No more sitting in the pantry doorway hoping you counted the cans correctly. Take your new list with you to the grocery store. After you have finished making your shopping list, put the menu cards back into the front of the file box to be used again.

Fun Extras

After you have gathered the basics, begin to add variety to your food storage. Plan for your family's specific needs. By incorporating family favorites, there will be no need for diet changes when you have to rely on your food storage. In fact ideally, your family should not even be able to tell that you are eating strictly out of your storage. As items go on sale, purchase a few extra. Best of all, these foods will rotate naturally, reducing the chances of spoilage or waste.

Plan to add seasonings and herbs to your food storage. These will make the food more palatable and add variety. This will also allow you to vary the planned menus you have on hand. If for instance, you have jars of applesauce on hand, but want something a bit different, you can add some cinnamon to the fruit and change the flavor slightly. Seasonings can also change the flavor of a basic food such as tomato sauce. With oregano it becomes an Italian food, add some crushed red peppers and it becomes a Mexican food.

Our food storage includes such foods as potato chips, soda, and candy. We did not add these foods to our storage however until all of our necessary foods had been stored. Chips will actually last about 6 months on the shelf. Because these are "extra" foods and not necessities, I don't attempt to keep a year supply of them on hand. These foods are just for fun, or for special occasions. Snacks that store well such as popcorn, gelatin and pudding are a staple in our food storage.

Our family enjoys eating cold cereal. Boxes of cereal stored in their original containers will stay fresh for about 6-12 months. Check the use by date on the box tops to ensure that you only buy what you can safely use before it goes stale. Cereal certainly isn't a necessity of life, but is a fun comfort food, especially if you have children. Cereal can be eaten without milk poured on it for a snack.

Another fun item that we have chosen to store is the powdered mix that makes ice cream. We have a little ice cream freezer. This mix can be added to reconstituted powdered milk, a jar of fruit and flavoring and then frozen to make ice cream. We have made this ice cream and it is very tasty. The chocolate mix is good, and the vanilla can have flavored syrups or fruit added to it to change the flavor. I keep boxes of non-dairy whipped topping powder on hand to make whipped cream substitute. Chocolate, strawberry and caramel syrups are also nice to have on hand and have a long shelf life.

We chose to add hard candies to our supply also. Hard candies have a long shelf life and store well in their original containers. A piece can help a craving for something sweet and help to keep you from feeling deprived if you are living off of your food storage. Chocolate hard candies keep well on the shelf for a few months, longer if they are in the freezer. Chocolate chips stored on the shelf or in the freezer can also be used as a sweet treat. Flavored baking chips can also be eaten as a treat. A few in the hand can be a sweet candy with a different flavor.

Butter flavored shortening can be used when baking goodies that require margarine. This will store on the shelf like regular shortening. Canned sweetened condensed milk is good to keep on hand for making cookies, fudge and other treats.

Peanut butter or oatmeal raisin cookies taste like a treat, but are a great way to get some nutrition in a fun snack.

Master mixes for cakes, cookies, pancakes, muffins and breads can cut down on the cost of convenience foods. These can be made up ahead from the staples that you buy and then stored in an airtight container on the shelf. One of my favorite cookbooks for master mixes is called "Make a Mix Cookery". Jell-O has a cookbook with wonderful ideas for gelatin and pudding desserts. Many major name brand food companies will send you recipes for free. Look online at their websites or write to them at the address listed on their packages.

If you are living off of your food storage, gifts from your kitchen are a fun idea for Holidays. In our family we make our Christmas gifts that to exchange with others. One Saturday before Christmas, all the women in our family get together for a baking day. We each bring ingredients from our food storage to one house, and spend the day cooking, baking and canning. Some past gifts have included jars of preserved fruits, meats and vegetables. We also make and give jars of cookie, brownie or cake mixes. This allows us to participate in gift exchanges while keeping costs in line. Not only do we have a gift of love to share with each other, we also have enough to share with our friends and neighbors.

Stretching Your Food Dollar

There are several things you can do to stretch your food dollar. Some of them take more time than others. With a bit of extra work though, you will reap the rewards of saving money.

Foods go on sale at different times of the year. Hamburger usually goes on sale in late May and late August. Turkey during November, roasts and chickens during the winter months. Canned vegetables go on sale in late October through late November and again in the spring. Sugar, flour and baking products are at their best prices several times during the winter holidays. Snack foods and party foods are least expensive just before school starts and between Christmas and New Year. Mexican foods go on sale the end of April through May 5th and again late August through the first week of September. Produce reaches its peak in the summer. Take advantage of these sales to stretch your food money.

Clip and use coupons for items that you are planning to buy. Young family members can clip and sort the coupons. You can find coupons online if you have access to the Internet. Coupons generally appear in the newspaper a few weeks before items go on sale at the supermarket. For example, you will find coupons for sweetened condensed milk in late October before it goes on sale with other baking items in early November. Coupons used on items that you don't really need or want wastes time and money. Add a coupon to an item on sale and increase your savings. By knowing what you need for a whole year, you can buy in bulk, on sale, with a coupon and not over purchase. Swap coupons with other friends and family members. This will increase the number of usable coupons for you and your friends. I use the money saved from coupons to purchase additional food for storage.

Sometimes purchasing in bulk will save you money. Items such as flour and sugar can be purchased in larger quantities and repackaged into usable amounts. Consider the cost of the materials you use in repackaging when deciding if it is cost efficient. Also check the expiration date of the product to see if you can use that much before it goes bad. Buying more than you need just because it looks like a bargain can lead to waste. Knowing how much you need for a full year will keep you from overbuying or under buying.

Start a family food co-op. Each family puts in a designated amount of money each month. The money is then used to purchase food in bulk. For example, each family puts $5.00 into the fund. The money can then be used to purchase a 50 pound bag of flour at a substantial discount. The food is then divided equally among all the families. Buying in larger quantities often results in saving money. It isn't always practical for individuals to buy large quantities of flour or sugar etc. Young or newly married family members may not have the financial resources to buy in bulk on their own. This way everyone benefits from the increased buying power.

Including the youngest families in an extended family food storage program ensures that they too will be taken care of in a time of need. It is important that these skills be passed down to each generation. Each member of the extended family has a unique perspective that will benefit the family as a whole. Every member has something to contribute to this important effort.

Another option is to grow part of the food that your family eats. Remember to include seeds in your food storage. Growing flowers won't provide you with food, however they will brighten your surroundings. For city dwellers or those living in apartments, gardening is still possible. Food can be grown in small pots or containers. Herbs, tomatoes and patio fruit trees can all be grown in containers. Consult your local County Extension Service for information on growing food in your area.

Consider starting a family garden with extended family members. If one family has a larger yard, or more patio space than the others, perhaps extended family members could help each other tend and harvest the food. Family time can be spent tending the common garden. Another possibility is for each family to grow one or two foods. One family can grow tomatoes and peas, while another family grows corn and green beans. Grow as much food as you reasonably can. At harvest time, share what you have grown, and everyone will have a variety of fresh produce.

Preserving what you grow can also be a family activity. Children can help to peel, cut and clean the produce. Adults can bottle, freeze or dehydrate the food. Growing your own food will help to ensure quality and freshness. Preserving foods at home will also stretch your dollar. There is an initial investment in supplies and equipment. Most of these supplies are reusable.

Home canning and preserving sounds like a daunting task. It is easier than it sounds. There are several good books on the market with clear step-by-step directions on how to home can. My personal favorite is the "Ball Blue Book Guide to Home Canning, Freezing and Dehydration". I can my own fruits, vegetables, soups, chili, and meats. A pressure canner is required to can meats. It is similar to, but not the same as a pressure cooker. Cooking and discount stores carry pressure canners. A deep pot for a water bath will allow you to can fruits and vegetables. A food dehydrator can be used to make jerky, fruit leathers, or vegetables. This is an excellent way to preserve food. Our family gets together to can food in bulk. We have an enjoyable time with each other while sharing the work.

Freezing is another option if you have the space available in a freezer. You can pour the food into freezer bags and freeze them flat. This will maximize the amount of food you can get into a small amount of space. Label and date everything. Food all looks the same when it is frozen. Food will not last as long in a freezer, but is easy and convenient. I would not recommend that you plan to freeze all of your meats, fruits and vegetables. In case of a power outage, the food could spoil. I do freeze some of my food. I dehydrate and can the rest of it.

It is possible to cook once and eat twice. For example, when you cook chili one night for dinner, make a double batch. Serve what you need for dinner, then either freeze the leftovers or pour it into jars and can it. It will only take a few minutes to pour it into jars, cap them and place them into the meat canner. Let it pressure can for 75 minutes while you do the dishes and get your evening chores done. Then you will have several jars of chili to put on your pantry shelf the next morning. This will work with other foods too such as soups and spaghetti sauces. If you cook once and eat twice, you will save time and money.

Plan ahead when you make your menus. For instance, if I plan to have a roast for dinner on Sunday, I cook a roast 3 times larger than needed for one meal. Then on Monday I shred the rest of the leftover roast. One half of the shredded roast gets barbecue sauce mixed with it for sandwiches. The other half gets salsa mixed in it to make a meat mix for chimichangas, shredded beef tacos or burros. Other ideas for leftover roast include vegetable beef soup or stew.

Many foods will lend themselves to this style of menu planning. You can cook all the hamburger you will need for a week at once. Separate it into meal-sized portions, wrap well and either freeze it or refrigerate it depending on how soon you plan to use it. The cooked hamburger can then be seasoned when you are ready to use it to make spaghetti, sloppy joes, tacos, casseroles, goulash, etc.

When we go on vacation, we take along jars of the food that we have canned. Cooking a few of our dinners in the hotel room saves us money. We open the jars, pour the contents into a bowl and reheat it in the microwave. This gives us a home cooked meal that is tasty and low cost. Home canned food can also be taken on camping trips. This is a great way to bring food from home that requires no refrigeration. We have taken along jars of chicken noodle soup, vegetable beef soup, chili, roast beef cubes (for shredding), fruits and vegetables.

Cooking from scratch will help to stretch your food money, although this will take considerable time. If you are willing to put forth the effort, you will reap the benefit of having more money to invest in your food storage.

To save time and reduce costs, consider making your own dry mixes for cookies, cakes, pancakes etc. Spend several hours making your own mixes and you will have low cost convenience foods for months at a fraction of the cost. These will store well on the shelf and are convenient. Store your mixes in an airtight container to retain freshness. Rotate them often, as these mixes usually last 3-6 months on the shelf. Store the ingredients to make mixes in your food storage. One morning making mixes can give you enough to make six months worth of meals. Homemade cookies and breads taste great and cost less than their store bought counterparts.

Look for generic brands or store brands and purchase these only when doing so won't affect flavor or use. Generics cost less, and usually are of the same quality as the name brand product. Be careful though, some products really do taste different. Generic peanut butter won't do you much good if your family refuses to eat it. When buying a new brand of a product, purchase a small quantity to try out the first time. This way you aren't stuck with a large quantity of something that your family won't eat.

Saving money will take extra time. Making it a game will make it easier. In our family, my daughters often compare their register receipts after they finish their grocery shopping and announce how much money they saved. We call each other to share information about deals we can take advantage of in the supermarket. I also get to hear what foods they are able to add to their food storage with the money they saved on their regular food bill. We get excited for each other when one of us does an exceptional job of stretching a dollar. It is fun to work together to save money and gather our food storage.

Family Involvement: Con the kids into helping

Let's face it, this is a huge hurdle. Not only do we have to gather and store a year's worth of food and goods to take care of our family, but get them to help too? This is probably not going to be the easiest part of the process. If you have children, it doesn't matter how young or old they are, it isn't too late to get them involved. Some ages and stages just require more creativity on your part to find ways to get them involved.

Share the responsibilities with your immediate family. Allow each member to choose a task. These tasks may include, but not limited to, making grocery lists, scanning food ads, clipping and sorting coupons, budgeting, and shopping. The children's ages and developmental stages should be taken into consideration as you divide up the work. For example, young children can help make a list of their favorite meals. This will help you to purchase foods your family enjoys. School age children can cut coupons and circle specials in the food ads. Teens can help you budget the money and shop. Find ways for the family to help while making sure that each chore is important. Working together as a family teaches responsibility and promotes a sense of belonging.

In our family, we divided the food storage chores up in creative ways. We tried to find ways to make it fun while teaching new skills. Each child was given a set amount of money, a stack of coupons and the weekly food ads. They were then encouraged to see how far they could stretch their money while purchasing their favorite foods. We also played "guess the total" where the children added the price of the food in their heads as we shopped. Other times they were given a calculator to help them figure out the unit price to help them determine the best bargain. This helped them to strengthen math, reading and sorting skills. Our family included foster children. We often had 4-6 children living in our family at a time. Ages ranged from infants to teens. At one point we had one toddler and four teenagers. Sometimes grocery shopping was an all morning event, but we considered it family time.

Once we arrived home with the food, children tended to scatter as far from the chores as possible. Then it was time for me to really get creative. I had to find ways to encourage my children to leave the fun of their toys and help me put away massive amounts of food. Food had to be repackaged into usable amounts, dated and put away correctly. I bought chips, cookies, candies and meats in large packages.

I always got the chore of repackaging the meats into meal-sized portions and putting them into the freezer. I let the children be in charge of repacking the snack foods. To make this more fun, I purchased a food scale. The children had fun weighing the food as they made up snack bags. By making it into a "factory production line" game we turned a chore into a fun family activity. More than a few chips and cookies were flavor tested by the nibble method while repackaging. Honestly, sometimes it would have been easier to just do it myself, but parenthood is about loving our children enough to teach them about work. The children enjoyed putting chips, cookies and snack foods into small sandwich sized plastic bags. These bags were then put into an airtight container and put into the pantry. This helped with portion control when one of them wanted a snack. It also made packing lunches a breeze. As the children packed their lunches, they would choose a snack bag to add to their lunchbox.

Now that my children are grown with their own families, we still sometimes do our grocery shopping together. Once a week we get together to swap coupons. We compare grocery lists too. If two or more of us need flour that week, we can buy a larger amount while cutting the unit price. When we get home, we divide up the chores of repacking the foods and then have lunch together.

Where to Store Your Food

When I first got married, we lived in a tiny one-bedroom apartment. We barely had room to store a toothbrush, which left no room for food storage. It wasn't that we owned a lot of possessions, this just happened to be a very small apartment. Food was put away in some rather strange places out of necessity. As our young family grew and became bigger, so did our living spaces. With that however came more possessions, so there still wasn't much room to store food.

Then came the day that all the children were grown. We had a five-bedroom home. I was able to use one whole bedroom, wall-to-wall, floor to ceiling for a food room. I also had the luxury of a full pantry, and a closet that had shelves. Oh what fun I had filling up all that space with food and supplies. I went wild shopping in bulk.

That luxury didn't last very long. We sold our house and moved to another one. The house was so cute and we fell in love with it. Reality however, hit hard after we tried to fit our food storage in the tiny new house. We no longer had an extra bedroom to use for food storage. I soon discovered that the darling cozy kitchen I had fallen in love with was woefully short on cabinets. Still, we loved the new house and decided to create storage where none had been before.

The first thing we did was to buy some freestanding storage cabinets. Two of these held an incredible amount of food. The house did have three hall closets. One I decided to use for

34

linens. The other two, my husband filled with deep shelves. He left space at the bottom of each closet for the five gallon buckets of staples. The other shelves hold canned goods and bottles of home canned food. Clear plastic bins hold the Mylar bags of food in an organized way. A master list told me where everything is stored until I got used to the new spaces.

Finding places to store your food may prove to be as big a challenge as obtaining it in the first place. Many of us live in places where we already utilize the space that we have to the maximum imaginable. With the help of our family, a bit of ingenuity and some careful searching, there may be some places you can still find to use.

Start by organizing the spaces you already use in your home for other things. Just doing this will likely free up some space that you didn't realize you had. Organize the children's toys and belongings. Organize and consolidate items in your closets. Install shelves or baskets to keep things organized once you have them where you want them. After this is done, look again at all the hidden spaces in your home to see if there is now extra room to store food.

Closets sometimes have only one shelf above the clothing rod. Check to see if a second shelf can safely be installed above it. This will increase storage space in that closet. Our bedroom closet is not very long but is about 15 inches deeper than a normal closet. We brought the clothing rod forward and installed shelves on the back of the closet wall. We still have room to hang our clothing but we can store food on the shelves behind the clothes. If you have to store food in out of the way places, make a master list of where the food is and tape it to the inside of a kitchen cupboard or pantry door. This will eliminate the hunt for food to refill canisters or pantry shelves.

Build and install shelves into existing coat or linen closets. Make them deep enough to hold several #10 cans. Place them far enough apart to be able to load food to the back of the shelf when you buy groceries. Always put the newest food in the back of the shelf so you use the oldest food first. This will help you rotate your food correctly. Group similar foods together, either by category such as baking or vegetables, or by placing all the canned goods on one shelf, jars on another etc. It is amazing how much food can be stored in one small coat closet. Date everything you buy so that you always know how old it is. This way, if a can of food doesn't get rotated you will still know if it is safe to eat.

Number 10 cans need to be stored up off the ground. They can be kept on shelves or on pallets. This will keep the cans away from water and rodents. There are commercial shelving units available at hardware stores that have an open weave shelf. They are made of high-grade plastic and will hold a large amount of weight without bowing.

Large quantities of food stored in 5 gallon buckets or in case lots, can be stored under beds. Always line your buckets with a food grade liner. Rodents can and will get into food that they smell. Oxygen packets can also be put into the buckets to lengthen shelf life of the food. Food stored in buckets or case lots can be more difficult to retrieve when you need to refill a shelf with the food. However, when space is limited, it will work.

Although foods may be stored under beds, it isn't recommended that you store food underneath waterbeds. These beds are often heated. Heat can make food unsafe to eat by promoting spoilage. It will also lessen the shelf life of the food. Storing food outside in a garage or shed is also unsafe. Food needs to be kept indoors in a cool, dry place. It is important that the temperature in your storage area be between 50 and 70 degrees Fahrenheit. Refrigerator foods should be less than forty degrees. Frozen foods need to be kept at 0 degrees.

If you have a couch or a loveseat up against a wall, move the furniture out from the wall a foot or two. Stack boxes of canned vegetables or jars behind the furniture. Cover the stack with a cloth and use it as a sofa table. Place a vase of flowers on top, a few table books or some decorative items. It will appear to be a piece of furniture and not a stack of food. Be careful to not stack the boxes too high, as this could be a safety hazard. If the boxes are accessible to children, never stack higher than your youngest child's head. Stack a few boxes in a column, place a tablecloth over it and use it as a nightstand or a lamp table. Look under existing nightstands and lamp tables you currently use to see if there is room to store a few boxes also. I realize that your goal probably isn't to decorate in "Early American Grocery Store", but with a bit of fabric you can disguise those potato pearls.

On the next few pages you will find a handy guide to the shelf life of foods. Tear this out or make a copy and tape it to the inside of your kitchen cabinet. This guide will help you to decide what the use by date is on the foods you put into storage. Your actual storage time may differ if you store foods above the recommended temperatures.

Food Storage Timetable

Biscuit, muffin mixes

Shelf: 9 months

Cereals

Ready-to-eat (unopened)

Shelf: 6-12 months

Ready-to-eat (opened)

Shelf: 2-3 months

Ready-to-cook oatmeal, etc.

Shelf: 12 months

Cornmeal

Shelf: 6-12months

Keep tightly closed. Refrigeration may prolong shelf life.

Flour

White

Shelf: 12-18 months

Whole Wheat

Shelf: 6-8 months

Both will store longer if stored with oxygen packets

Grits

Shelf: 12 months

Yeast (dry)

Shelf: Expiration date on package.

Keep dry and cool

Pancake mixes

Shelf: 9-12 months

Pasta

Shelf: 2 years

Rice

White

Shelf: 2 years

Brown

Shelf: 1 year

Mixes

Shelf: 6 months

Butter, Margarine

Refrigerator: 1-2 months

Freezer: 12 months.

Cheese

Hard and wax coated Cheddar, Edam, Gouda, Swiss, brick, etc.

Unopened

Refrigerator: 3-6 months

Freezer: 12 months

Milk

Evaporated or Condensed Milk

Unopened

Shelf: 12 months

Opened

Refrigerator: 1 week

Invert can every 2 months. Cover tightly.

Nonfat dry, not reconstituted

Unopened

Shelf: 12 months

Will store longer if tightly sealed with oxygen packets

Opened

Shelf: 6 months

Refrigeration may prolong quality.

Fish

Fatty fish (mackerel, trout, salmon, etc.)

Freezer: 2-3 months

Lean fish (cod, flounder, etc.)

Freezer: 6 months

Breaded, frozen

Freezer: 3 months

Canned (all kinds and juices)

Bottled

Shelf: 12 months

Frozen fruit concentrate

Home Frozen or Purchased Frozen

Freezer: 12 months

Meat

Chops

Freezer: 9-12 months

Ground

Freezer: 9-12 months

Roast

Freezer: 9-12 months

Sausage

Freezer: 1-2 months

Steaks

Freezer: 9-12 months

Stew Meat

Freezer: 9-12 months

Chicken

Fresh—Whole

Freezer: 12 months

Fresh—Pieces

Freezer: 6-9 months

Canned-Unopened

Shelf: 12 months

Baking Powder, Soda

Shelf: 18 months

Bouillon Cubes, Granules

Shelf: 2 years

Catsup, Chili Sauce, Barbeque Sauce (unopened)

Shelf: 12 months

Chocolate

Shelf: 12 months

May "bloom" but is safe to use

Chocolate Syrup

Shelf: 2 years

Cornstarch

Shelf: 18 months

Gelatin

Shelf: 18 months

Honey

Shelf: 12 months

Jams, Jellies

Shelf: 12 months

Marshmallows

Shelf: 3-6 months

Creme

Shelf: 2-3 months

Mayonnaise

Shelf: 6-12 months

Molasses

Shelf: 12 months

Mustard, prepared yellow

Shelf: 2 years

Oils

Shelf: 18 months

Pectin

Shelf: 18 months

Peanut Butter

Shelf: 12 months

Salad Dressings

Bottled

Shelf: 10-12 months

Shortening

Shelf: 1 year

Spices and Herbs

Ground Pieces

Shelf: 12 months

Herbs

Shelf: 12 months

Sugar

Brown (sealed)

Shelf: 12-18 months

Confectioners

Shelf: 18 months

Granulated

Shelf: 2 years

Sweetner, artificial

Shelf: 2 years

Syrup

Shelf: 12 months

Vanilla

Unopened

Shelf: 2 years

Opened

Shelf: 12 months

Vinegar

Unopened

Shelf: 2 years

Opened

Shelf: 12 months

Canned Vegetables

All types

Shelf: 1 year

Frozen

Commercially frozen

Freezer: 8-12 months

Home frozen

Freezer: 1 year

Baby Food, canned

Shelf: 1 year

Cake, Cookie Mixes

Shelf: 1 year

Crackers

Shelf: 6-12 months

Popcorn-Unpopped

Shelf: 2 years

Pudding mixes

Shelf: 1 year

Sauces, Condiments, etc.

Hot sauce, Worcesterhire etc.

Shelf: 18 months to 2 years

Salsa

12-18 months

<u>Family 72 Hour Kit</u>

An important part of your food storage and readiness plan is the 72-hour kit. This kit will need to have everything you need to care for your family comfortably for approximately 3 days. Each person should be able to carry their own backpack or bag of items with them. In our family each person has a personal 3 day kit in a backpack. Then we also have a family kit that has more comfort items in it. These are not as essential, but would make our lives more comfortable if we had them. In case of a natural disaster, it can take several days for relief agencies to reach the disaster area. Having a 72-hour kit will ease the stress and discomfort for your family.

We store the family kit in an accessible place. This kit can be easily loaded into a car by anyone in our family. Each person also keeps a personal 3 day kit handy. The trunk of each car in the family also has an emergency kit. We keep an emergency blanket, water, food, flares, flashlight, first aid kit and repair tools in the kit. This kit can be stored in a small bag or in a #10 can. These supplies don't take up much room. However, in case the car breaks down, we would be comfortable until help arrives.

As a family, talk about the natural disasters that happen in your area. Formulate a plan of action to deal with those emergencies. Different parts of the country have different natural disasters. My family lives in a low desert in Arizona. We don't get hurricanes or tornados. We do however get floods from time to time. When it rains, the ground is so dry that the water doesn't soak in and it floods. We had to plan our disaster drills around this probable emergency. People in other parts of our state deal with things like forest fires. They sometimes get only a few minutes notice before being evacuated.

Our area also has a lot of power outages during storms. Power can be out for a few hours to several days. Our kitchen has an electric oven and stove so cooking during a power outage requires other methods. We have included alternate fuels to cook our food as well as foods that don't require cooking. Cooking can be done on the gas barbecue grill in the backyard if our power is out. The grill is not portable however so it can't be counted on in a three-day kit if we have to evacuate. We have a small propane camp stove that we can take with us, as well as sterno fuel. The sterno fuel is lightweight, easy to carry and will cook small amounts of food.

When an evacuation takes place, it can be hard to decide what to take with you. Keep a checklist handy in your family three-day kit. Include on the list things that you would like to take if there is time. For example, you might want to take copies of important documents, special pictures, extra food, comfort items etc. We keep all our negatives from photos and originals of documents in a fireproof safe in our house. That way if there is a flood or a fire and our house is destroyed, we will still have photos and documents.

Plan a place to meet. This way if your family is separated, everyone will be trying to get to the same place. Communication may be hampered during an emergency. If you have to leave home, leave a note clearly stating where you are headed and what time you left. Also include the names of everyone you are taking with you. This is important information for anyone that comes looking for you.

Each member of the family can provide input as to what would make them comfortable in case of an emergency. Then the family can gather and pack their three day kits, and choose where to store them. Consider items such as medications, diapers and special dietary needs. Be sure to rotate the food in each kit so that it remains fresh. Sample sizes of comfort items are available at the store. These wont take up much space, but will make a difference in emotional comfort during a crisis. Gather and pack the essentials first. Then, if there is room, pack the comfort items. We included small travel games, notepaper and pens. If you have pets, include food and water for them. Each family's list will be different and will reflect the needs within their own family.

See the example lists to get ideas for your own family kits. Adjust the list to fit your own family's needs. Pack the supplies in a container that is lightweight enough to be picked up and carried to the car. One idea is to pack the supplies in a garbage can on wheels. We keep ours in a bin that is on wheels. The family kit could also be placed in several smaller containers for ease of movement. Write on the outside of each container what is inside and what number that container is. For example, container number one has cooking supplies and is #1 out of 3 containers. This way you won't accidentally leave a container behind. Another idea is to place all emergency supplies in colored coded bins or containers. One glance will locate all the supplies. Each member of the family should know where the kits are located and how to get them to the car.

Family 72 Hour Kit Checklist

___ Tent

___ Sleeping bags

___ Camp stove

___ Propane tank

___ Matches

___ Knife

___ First aid kit

___ Water and purification tablets

___ Dishes, Silverware

___ Pots and Pans

___ Potholders

___ Garbage bags

___ Dishtowel

___ Wash cloth

___ Dish soap

___ Can opener

___ Porta potti

___ Toilet paper

___ Hand soap

___ Pencil and paper

___ Documents (copies only)

___ Cash

___ Scriptures

___ Cereal

___ Granola bars

___ Juice

___ Soup

___ Crackers

___ Fruit cups

___ Beef stew

___ Chicken

___ Rice

___ Chili

___ Canned Vegetables

___ Canned Fruit

Personal 72 Hour Kit

___ One change of clothing

___ Solar blanket

___ Flashlight

___ Batteries

___ Toiletries

___ Tissue

___ Cash, change

___ Garbage bags

___ String, twine

___ Knife, scissors

___ Hand towel

___ Washcloth

___ Plastic silverware

___ Paper and pencil

___ Dust mask

___ First aid kit

Food

___ Granola bars

___ Cheese and crackers

___ Fruit cups

___ Water

___ Juice boxes

___ Tuna kit

___ Hard candy

___ Dry cereal

Emergency Car Kit

2 empty #10 cans lined with a plastic bag, fitted lid

Can #1

Can opener

2 candles

Compass

First aid kit

Notepad, pen, pencil

Matches

2 thirty gallon plastic bags

Sewing kit

Hand towel

String

Dust mask

Army knife

Toilet paper

Triangle bandage or bandana

Twisty ties

Small roll wire

Envelope with extra cash and change

Flashlight, batteries

Duct tape

<u>Can #2</u>

Non perishable food i.e.:

Granola bars

Peanut butter on crackers

Fruit rollups

Dry cereal

Dried fruit

Cookies

Pre packaged snacks (nuts, pretzels etc)

Water or juice in half-pint containers

And Finally….

The final pages of this workbook include recipes, sample menus and blank menus for you to fill out. The blank menus include spaces for breakfast, lunch, dinner and two snacks. Only fill out those meals and snacks that your family eats. Use these worksheets as a guideline. Change them to fit your needs and personalize the system. If your family eats seven different meals, then you will only need to fill out one week of menus. If they routinely eat 14 meals, then fill out two menu sheets. Our family eats 31 different meals so I needed to fill out 5 sheets of menus, including holiday meals. Once you begin writing down everything your family eats, you may find that you have more options than you first thought.

Now it is time to begin the work. Make a plan. Use a notebook to write down small, reachable goals. Track your progress. Reward your accomplishments. Share what you know with others. Talk to friends and gain from their knowledge and experience. Once you know what you need, this task will be less overwhelming than thinking that you need to go out and gather a year's worth of food all at once. Keep track of what you have purchased to avoid duplication. Being organized will save you time. Careful planning will save you money. Relax and have fun with this. Gathering and storing a year supply will bring you the blessing of comfort and peace of mind. It is well worth the work and the effort. In times of personal trial, or in the event of a natural disaster, you will be able to take care of your family comfortably.

Recipes

Sometimes coming up with interesting, tasty and nutritious meals at the end of an already too long day is just more work than it seems to be worth. So, there we stand, staring into the pantry, refrigerator and freezer, wishing that by some miracle the food would prepare itself. Menu planning eliminates the 4:00 P.M. glazed over look. This section has our family favorites using food from our food storage. You can use frozen meats or home canned. The same is true for the vegetables. These recipes were chosen because they are inexpensive and easy to prepare.

Some of the recipes for the desserts and snacks listed on the sample menu sheets can be found in the Jell-O brand Fun and Fabulous Recipes cookbook. Boxes of gelatin and pudding store well on the shelf for long periods of time and are delicious treats.

Many of the recipes listed in this section these can be made ahead and frozen for those nights when you need an extra fast meal on the table. Many of the main dish foods can be prepared in a crock-pot for added convenience. Enjoy!

<u>Barbecued Beef</u>

2 or 3 lb roast

½ onion chopped

1 bottle barbecue sauce

Place roast, onion and barbecue sauce into slow cooker. Slow cook on high for 4-6 hours or until meat is tender and shreds easily. Shred meat. Serve over steamed rice or on toasted buns. Serves 8.

Steak Soup

1 lb steak cut into cubes

1 t steak seasoning

1 onion diced

1 bell pepper diced

4 potatoes cut into large chunks

4 carrots sliced

mixed vegetables of your choice

Sprinkle steak with seasoning. Brown steak in a small amount of hot oil in skillet. Put browned meat, onion, bell pepper, potatoes, carrots and mixed vegetables into 8-10 cups boiling water. Simmer for 1 ½ - 2 hours till meat is tender. To cook in a crock pot, put on high for 4 hours or 7 hours on low. Serves 6.

<u>Stew</u>

1 pound cubed stew meat, roast or steak

8 c water

1 small onion chopped

4 potatoes cubed

4 carrots sliced into coins

½ c celery

3 c assorted mixed vegetables

Garlic powder, onion powder, salt, pepper to taste

Oil for frying

1 c flour

1t Kitchen Bouquet

Stir together the flour, garlic powder, onion powder, salt and pepper. Split the flour into two dishes of ½ c each. Use one dish to dredge the meat and set aside the remaining flour to make gravy after the roast is finished. Dredge meat in ½ c of the flour mixture. Brown the meat in hot oil on all sides. Place browned meat in boiling water in large soup pot. Bring back to boil. Simmer for two hours till meat is tender, adding water as needed. Add remaining ingredients. Simmer for 30 minutes longer till vegetables are tender. Add the remaining ½ c of the flour to 1 c cool water. Stir until lump free. Add 1 t kitchen bouquet and stir well. Slowly add to the boiling stew. Simmer until the gravy thickens. To cook in a crock-pot, add browned meat to hot water in pot. Add vegetables and cook on high 4 hours, or on low 8 hours till meat is tender. Serves 6

Juli Brown

<u>Vegetable Beef Soup</u>

1 lb stew beef cubed

1 onion chopped

4 potatoes cubed

4 carrots sliced into coins

1 (16 oz) can tomatoes

16 oz frozen mixed vegetables

salt and pepper to taste

Add stew beef and onions to boiling salted water. Boil for 1½ hours till meat is tender. Add remaining ingredients and Simmer for 30 minutes till tender. To cook in a crock-pot, place beef, onions, and vegetables in crock-pot filled with water. Cook on high for 4 hours or low for 8 hours. Serves 6

<u>Beef and Gravy</u>

1½ lbs ground beef

½ onion chopped

½ t garlic powder

½ c flour

1 c water

1 t Kitchen Bouquet

Brown ground beef with onions and garlic powder. Stir in flour and brown lightly. Wisk in 2 cups water and stir well. Stir in Kitchen Bouquet liquid gravy seasoning. Simmer till thickened. Pour over mashed potatoes or noodles.

Swiss Pepper Steak

2-3 lbs round steak cut into cubes

1 pkt swiss pepper steak seasoning mix

2 cans chopped tomatoes

1 small onion chopped

1 green bell pepper, chopped

1 red bell pepper, chopped

flour

salt and pepper to taste

oil for frying

Dredge steak cubes in flour. Brown steak cubes and onions in skillet with small amount of hot oil. Brown on all sides. Drain any oil left from pan. Add water to cover one inch over the meat. Stir in pepper steak seasoning packet. Add onion, bell peppers and tomatoes. Bring to a boil and simmer for 1 hour till meat is tender adding small amounts of water as needed to keep meat covered. Serve over mashed potatoes or rice. To cook in crock-pot, dredge meat in flour and brown in hot oil with onions. Add browned meat onions, bell peppers, tomatoes and seasoning packet to crock-pot. Cover with water. Place lid on top and cook for 4 hours on high, 8 hours on low. Serves 6-8.

Hamburger Noodle Casserole

1 lb Hamburger

¼ cup dehydrated or ½ cup chopped fresh onions

8 ounces pasta any shape

2 (8oz) cans tomato sauce

1 (16 oz) can tomatoes

¼ t garlic powder

½ t salt

¼ t pepper

4 slices American cheese or 2 ounces shredded cheese

Boil pasta according to package directions. Brown hamburger with onions. Drain fat. Stir together the cooked hamburger, cooked pasta and remaining ingredients except cheese. Heat through. Top with shredded cheese or cheese slices if desired. Serves 6.

<u>Sloppy Joes</u>

1 lb hamburger

¼ c dehydrated onions

1 packet sloppy joe seasoning

2 cans (8 oz) tomato sauce

¼ t granulated sugar

4 hamburger buns or rolls

Brown hamburger and onions. Drain well. Stir in sloppy joe seasoning packet, tomato sauce and sugar. Simmer for 10 minutes till thickened. Serve on toasted hamburger buns. Serves 4.

Meatloaf

1 ½ lbs hamburger

½ c dehydrated onions

1 can condensed tomato soup

1 egg beaten

½ c milk

½ cup fine cracker crumbs

½ t salt

¼ t pepper

1/8 t garlic powder

1 T Worcestershire sauce or steak sauce

Mix all ingredients well. Shape into loaf in shallow baking pan. Bake 1 hour at 375 degrees F. Drain fat and serve. Serves 4-6

Chili

1 lb hamburger

½ c dehydrated onions

1 pkg chili seasoning mix

1 can (26-30 oz) ranch style beans

1 (16 oz) can pinto beans

2 (8 oz) cans tomato sauce

1 (16 oz) can tomatoes

1 can diced green chilies

Brown hamburger with onions. Drain fat. Add other ingredients. Simmer for 15 minutes till heated through stirring occasionally. Serves 6

<u>Porcupine Meatballs</u>

1 lb hamburger

¼ c dehydrated onions

1 egg slightly beaten

1 cup cooked rice

1 can condensed tomato soup

salt and pepper to taste

Mix all ingredients together well. Shape into 16 meatballs. Brown in non stick skillet till cooked through, turning frequently. Serves 4.

Tacos

1 ½ lb hamburger

1 taco seasoning packet

¼ c dehydrated onions

salt and pepper to taste

8 corn tortillas

½ c cooking oil

4 oz shredded cheese (can use melted or reconstituted dehydrated cheese)

Garden fresh lettuce shredded and tomatoes, chopped

Brown the ground beef with the onions, drain fat. Stir in the taco seasoning packet, salt pepper and mix well. Fry corn tortillas till semi crisp. Layer the ground beef, cheese, lettuce and tomatoes into the cooked corn tortillas. Serves 4

Enchiladas

8 corn tortillas

16 oz shredded longhorn or colby cheese

One 30 oz can enchilada sauce

½ med sized onion chopped

1 small can green chilies

½ c vegetable oil

Shredded lettuce

One chopped tomato

Heat oil in small skillet. Fry corn tortillas one at a time until softened in hot oil, about 10 seconds per side. Drain on paper toweling. Pour enchilada sauce into a sauce pan. Add onions and green chilies, heat till mixture boils. Dip a tortilla into the sauce, coating both sides. Lay tortilla flat on a plate. Place one ounce of shredded cheese on the lower third of tortilla. Roll into a tube shape, place seam side down in a baking dish. Repeat with remaining tortillas. Pour remaining sauce over top of rolled tortillas and top with the rest of the cheese. Bake at 400° F about 15-20 minutes or until cheese is melted. Serve with shredded lettuce and chopped tomatoes. Serves 4.

Green Chili Burro

2 c cooked shredded roast beef or cooked hamburger

½ med onion chopped

1 small can diced green chilies

1/8 t garlic powder

1 cup water or beef broth

3-4 T flour

vegetable oil for frying

4 oz shredded colby or longhorn cheese

shredded lettuce

chopped tomatoes

4 large flour tortillas

Mix flour and water or beef broth till smooth. Pour into saucepan and heat. Add in meat, green chilies and garlic powder, stir well. Heat till thickened. Place ½ cup meat mixture in center of large flour tortilla. Fold lower third up over the middle, fold in both sides, then roll into a tube shape. Fry in hot oil till golden brown. Top with shredded cheese, lettuce and tomatoes. Serve with salsa. Serves 4.

Fajitas

3 lbs top sirloin steak thinly sliced

2 green bell peppers

2 red bell peppers

2 yellow bell peppers

1 red or yellow onion

1 small can green chilies

Salt and pepper to taste

1 pkt fajita seasoning mix

12 small flour tortillas

Thinly slice peppers and onions. Mix together the meat, peppers, onion, chilies, salt, pepper and seasoning mix. Stir-fry in hot skillet with small amount of oil till meat is tender and cooked through. Spoon mixture into warm flour tortillas. Serves 4-6

Chimichangas

2 c shredded roast beef

1 small jar of salsa

1/2 small onion chopped

2 T finely chopped cilantro

4 oz shredded colby or longhorn cheese

4 large flour tortillas

shredded lettuce

chopped tomatoes

vegetable oil for frying

guacamole

sour cream

Mix shredded beef with salsa, onion, and cilantro. Heat in small saucepan or in microwave till hot. Place ½ c beef on center of flour tortilla. Fold lower third of tortilla up over center. Fold both sides in. Roll into a tube shape. Fry in hot oil till golden brown on all sides. Top with shredded cheese, lettuce, tomatoes, guacamole and sour cream. To make enchilada style, pour enchilada sauce over the fried chimichanga. Then top with cheese, lettuce, tomatoes, guacamole and sour cream. Serves 4.

Tostadas

6 corn tortillas

½ c vegetable oil

1 – 30 oz can refried beans

8 oz shredded colby or longhorn cheese

shredded lettuce

chopped tomatoes

chopped onions

salsa

Fry both sides of corn tortillas in hot oil till crisp. Drain well. Spread warmed refried beans over top of tortilla. Sprinkle onions, cheese, lettuce, tomatoes over top of beans. Serves 3-4.

Stuffed Quesadillas

2 c shredded beef

1 small jar salsa

½ small onion chopped (or dehydrated onion)

8 oz shredded cheese

¼ c finely chopped cilantro (if desired)

1 small can diced green chilies

4 large flour tortillas

Sour cream

Lettuce

Tomatoes

Guacamole

Mix shredded beef with salsa, onions, cilantro and green chilies. Heat through. Sprinkle 1 oz shredded cheese over one half of the flour tortilla. Sprinkle ½ c shredded beef mixture sporadically onto the same half of the flour tortilla. Fold the tortilla over the meat/cheese. Grill on hot oiled griddle till lightly browned. Flip and brown the other side. Cut into wedges. Garnish with salsa, lettuce, tomatoes, guacamole and sour cream.

Taco Salad

1 lb ground beef

¼ c dehydrated onions

1 pkt taco seasoning mix

1 16oz can refried beans

4 oz shredded colby or longhorn cheese

4 oz container of sour cream

4 oz container of guacamole

1 small jar salsa

shredded lettuce

1 tomato chopped

1 small bag of tortilla chips or corn chips

Brown ground beef with onions. Heat refried beans. Add seasoning packet. Drain fat. Place tortilla chips or corn chips on plate. Layer refried beans, ground beef, cheese, guacamole, sour cream, salsa, lettuce and tomatoes on top of chips. Serves 4.

Bean Burros

4 flour tortillas

1 – 30 oz can refried beans

1 small can of green chilies

¼ c chopped onions

4 oz shredded cheese

sour cream

guacamole

Spread refried beans across bottom third or flour tortilla. Top with green chilies, onion and cheese. Roll tortilla, folding in the sides to form a tube shape. Top with sour cream and guacamole.

Fry Bread

4 c flour

1 ½ t salt

4 t baking powder

4 T shortening

1 ½ - 2 c water

Sift dry ingredients together. Cut in shortening till coarse and crumbly. Add enough water to make a soft non-sticky dough. Knead gently till pliable. Roll into small balls. Flatten to ¼ inch thick. Let rise for about 10 minutes. Drop gently into hot oil and fry until puffy and lightly browned. Turn and brown other side. Drain well. Serve topped with either powdered sugar, honey or top with refried beans and cheese like a tostada.

Chicken ala King

2 cups cooked cut up chicken

2 cans condensed cream of chicken soup

½ c milk

8 oz mixed vegetables

4 cups cooked rice

Heat chicken, soup, milk and vegetables in saucepan. Spoon over hot cooked rice or biscuits. Serves 4.

Chicken Noodle (or Rice) Soup

8 oz chicken (boneless, or precook chicken and remove bones before adding other ingredients)

6 c water or broth

3 chicken bouillon cubes

2 carrots cut up or ½ cup dehydrated carrots

1 stalk celery cut up or 1 T dehydrated celery

½ small onion chopped or ¼ cup dehydrated onions

4 oz wide egg noodles or 1 c white rice

salt and pepper to taste

Place chicken, carrots, celery and onion into salted water and bring to boil. Simmer one hour till chicken and vegetables are tender. Add egg noodles and boil for 10-12 minutes more. Broth can be thickened into gravy if desired with 3 T flour mixed with 1 c cool water. Slowly stir in the flour mixture into soup pot and heat till thickened. You can substitute a one-quart jar of home canned chicken or one can of store bought cooked chicken for the raw chicken. This will speed up making the soup. Add the cooked chicken to the bouillon cubes, water, carrots, celery and onions. Bring mixture to boil, add the egg noodles and cook for 10-12 minutes. Serves 6

Chicken and Rice Casserole

1 c cooked cut up chicken (pint jar or small can will also work)

2 ¼ c chicken broth (or 2 ¼ cups water and 2 chicken flavored bouillon cubes)

2 c instant white rice

¼ c dehydrated onions

1 c mixed vegetables if desired (can also use dehydrated carrots or a package of instant vegetable soup mix)

Heat chicken broth to boiling (or water and bouillon cubes). Add 2 c instant rice, chicken, onions, (and mixed vegetables if desired) stir well. Simmer for five minutes on low heat till rice absorbs the water. Serves 4.

Creamy Chicken and Rice Casserole

1 cup cooked cut up chicken (pint jar or small can will also work)

2 ¼ c chicken broth (or 2 ¼ c water with 2 chicken bouillon cubes)

2 c instant white rice

¼ c dehydrated onions

1 c mixed vegetables (if desired)

1 can condensed cream of chicken soup

Heat chicken broth to boiling (or water and bouillon cubes). Add the rest of the ingredients and stir well. Heat on low simmer for five minutes till rice is cooked through. Serves 4.

Chicken and Pasta

1 c cooked cut up chicken (pint jar or small can will also work)

1 4-5 oz box of pasta (such as Pasta Roni) any flavor

8 oz bag of frozen vegetables (i.e.: broccoli, cauliflower or carrots)

Cook pasta according to package directions. Add cut up chicken and vegetables. Heat thoroughly. Serves 2-3.

Chicken Pot Pie

1 c cooked cubed chicken

2 cans cream of chicken condensed soup

½ c milk

8 oz frozen (cook before adding to mixture) or 16 oz canned mixed vegetables

2 frozen pie crusts

Salt and pepper to taste

Combine the chicken, soup, milk, vegetables, salt and pepper. Pour into pie pan lined with pie crust. Top with remaining crust. Slit top in several places. Bake at 375 for 40 minutes till golden brown. Serves 4.

Chicken Salad

One can cooked chicken, or one pint jar home canned chicken shredded

2 T mayonnaise or salad dressing

1 t Mrs. Dash

¼ c chopped onions

½ c chopped lettuce

¼ c chopped celery

½ c chopped tomatoes

Shred chicken and stir in mayonnaise until well coated. Toss in the rest of the ingredients. Serve on bread or with crackers. Serves 3-4

Sweet and Sour Chicken

One pound boneless chicken cut into strips

½ cup onion sliced

1 cup red bell peppers

1 cup green bell peppers

1 cup drained pineapple chunks

1 bottle sweet and sour sauce

2 cups cooked rice

Sauté boneless chicken in large skillet till cooked through and no pink is left. Add onions and peppers and stir-fry until vegetables are tender crisp. Add pineapple and sweet and sour sauce and heat through. Serve over cooked rice. Serves 3-4

Tuna Salad

8 oz bag of corkscrew pasta

1 can tuna in water

¼ c mayonnaise or salad dressing

½ c chopped tomatoes

¼ c chopped celery

1 t Mrs. Dash seasoning

½ c shredded lettuce

Cook pasta in boiling salted water according to package directions. Drain, rinse and cool pasta. Drain tuna well. Stir in tuna and mayonnaise. Add remaining ingredients and chill well. Serve with crackers.

Pork Chop Bake

4 pork chops

1 can cream of mushroom soup

4 slices onion

2 c cooked rice

Pan fry pork chops till brown on both sides. Stir together the rice and soup mix. Put rice mixture into a glass baking dish. Top with pork chops and onion rings. Bake at 375 for 15 minutes.

Vegetable Rice Casserole

2 c instant rice

1 package Mrs. Grass vegetable soup mix (dry)

2 ½ cups salted water

½ lb browned ground beef

¼ c chopped onion

Brown ground beef and onion together, drain well. Bring water to boil. Add vegetable soup mix and rice. Stir together. Put lid on pan and remove from heat. Let sit for five minutes and stir in ground beef. Serves 4.

Pork and Beans

2 cans (16 oz each) pork and beans

4 hot dogs thinly sliced

¼ small onion chopped (or ¼ c dehydrated onions)

1 c tomato ketchup

½ c brown sugar

1 T prepared mustard

1 T Worcestershire sauce

Sauté hot dogs with onions till slightly browned, stirring often. Add remaining ingredients and simmer for 15 minutes.

<u>Grandma Wallis' Baked Beans</u>

1 Three pound can beans

1 med onion chopped

1 large green pepper, seeded and chopped

½ c brown sugar

1 T liquid smoke

½ c Ketchup

6-8 strips bacon

Mix all ingredients together using half the bacon diced, reserve the rest. Pour bean mixture into 13x9x2 inch pan. Top beans with remaining bacon. Bake at 275° F for 4 hours. Serves 6-8.

Chili Beans

1 lb dry beans

1 onion, diced

1 package chili seasoning

1 can chopped tomatoes

1 small can diced green chilies

½ t salt

Sort and rinse beans. Put beans in 8 cups water. Bring to a boil. Boil for 2 minutes. Turn off heat and let beans soak for one hour. Drain and rinse beans again. Put beans, onion, chili seasoning, tomatoes, green chilies and salt into 7 cups water. Bring to boil. Simmer for 1 ½ to 2 hours till beans are tender. Serves 6.

<u>Empanadas</u>

One can fruit pie filling (or 1 qt home canned fruit)

4 large flour tortillas

½ c powdered sugar

oil for frying

Place one large spoonful of fruit in center of flour tortilla. Fold lower half of tortilla up over the filling. Fold in both sides and roll from the bottom into a tube shape. Fry in hot oil till all sides are lightly browned. Drain well on paper toweling. Sprinkle with powdered sugar and serve warm or with ice cream. Store leftovers in the refrigerator. May be served cold. Serves 4.

Brownies

1 c margarine, melted

2 c white sugar

1 c flour

2/3 cup cocoa

2 eggs

½ t baking powder

½ c milk

1 ½ t vanilla

Mix all ingredients in a large bowl, beat well. Pour into greased 9x13 inch pan. Bake at 350 for 40 minutes or until brownies begin to pull away from sides.

Chocolate Frosting

12 oz chocolate chips (any flavor)

1 can sweetened condensed milk

Stir together over low heat in small saucepan stirring constantly. When melted, pour immediately over cooled brownies. Work quickly to spread. Cool to set frosting.

Cake Mix Cookies

1 box cake mix (any flavor)

½ c vegetable oil

1 egg

1/2 –3/4 c water

Stir together the cake mix, oil and egg. Add just enough water to moisten mixture and to make a very thick batter. Drop by spoonfuls onto greased cookie sheet. Bake at 350 F for 20-30 minutes till cookies spring back when touched. Remove from sheet and cool. Frost with your choice of icing.

Apple Cobbler With Crumb Topping

1 quart jar sliced cooked apples or can of pie filling

2 t cinnamon

Sugar to taste

1 T cornstarch

Stir together 1 cup juice from the jar of apples (or 1 c water) and the cornstarch in a small saucepan. Boil 1 minute stirring constantly and then add the fruit. Pour into 9x9 inch baking dish. Top with crumb topping. Bake at 400° F for 15 minutes. You can substitute any jar of home canned fruit for the apples. You can also substitute dehydrated apple slices by reconstituting them first. You may need to add a little bit more sugar if you use dehydrated apple slices.

Crumb Topping

½ c butter or margarine

¼ c packed brown sugar

1 c flour

Mix together with pastry blender. Drop in small dollops over the cobbler mixture. Bake at 400° F for 15 minutes.

Chocolate No Bake Cookies

½ c cocoa

1 stick margarine

2 c sugar

¼ c milk

1 t vanilla

½ c peanut butter

3 c quick oats

Melt together cocoa, sugar, milk and margarine. Boil for 1 minute. Stir in vanilla and peanut butter. Add Oatmeal and stir. Drop by spoonfuls onto cookie sheet. Cool and let set for two hours.

Microwave Caramel Corn

1 cube margarine

1 c brown sugar

¼ c white Karo syrup

¼ teaspoon baking soda

12 cups popped corn (butter flavored microwave popcorn is really good in this)

2 c cocktail peanuts (optional)

Combine margarine, brown sugar and syrup in a microwave safe dish. Cook in microwave on high for 2-3 minutes. Stir. Cook 1-2 minutes more, stirring each minute. Stir baking soda into mixture until blended and frothy. (It will foam so make sure your dish is deep) Pour liquid over popped corn and peanuts, stir until well coated. Pour popcorn onto a large cookie sheet. Bake in 250° F oven for one hour, stirring often. Instead of baking the popcorn in the oven, you can put the popcorn into a large paper bag. Close the bag, shake well. Microwave on high for 1 ½ minutes. Shake well again. Microwave on high for 1 minute. Shake well. Pour out onto a wax paper lined cookie sheet and cool.

Microwave Peanut Brittle

1 c white granulated sugar

½ c white Karo brand syrup

1 c (12 oz pkg) raw peanuts

1 t margarine or butter

1 t vanilla

1 t baking soda

Grease a large cookie sheet. (I use butter to grease it instead of shortening for flavor.) Place the sugar and the syrup into a deep microwave safe glass bowl. Microwave on high for approximately 4 minutes. Add the peanuts, stir and cook on high for two more minutes. Add margarine and vanilla. Stir. Cook on high for 1 minute. Add baking soda and stir well. It will get foamy and raise up the sides of the bowl. Make sure your bowl is deep enough. Pour onto greased cookie sheet. Cool and break into pieces.

Sweetened Condensed Milk

½ c butter or margarine (1 stick)

2 c white sugar

2 c non-fat dry milk

1 c boiling water

Place all ingredients in blender and blend until smooth. Pour into quart jar and store covered in the refrigerator. Mixture thickens up as it cools. Will store refrigerated for up to one week. Makes 3 cups milk. (14 oz can has 1 ¼ c milk in it.)

<u>Powdered sugar</u>

Blend one cup white granulated sugar on high speed in blender for 45 seconds. Check, if it isn't powdered enough blend again in five-second increments until fluffy.

Brown Sugar

Add 2 Tablespoons molasses to 1 cup of granulated white sugar. Mix well. Store tightly covered.

FOOD STORAGE
DAILY MENU RECORD

	Sunday	Monday	Tuesday	Wednesday	Thursday	Friday	Saturday
Breakfast	blueberry muffin milk	pumpkin bread milk	cream of wheat Raisins Milk	strawberry muffins milk	banana bread milk	blueberry pancakes milk	cold cereal toast Milk
Lunch	bean w/bacon soup cheese crackers	haystacks tortilla chips beans, cheese onions, chilies	turkey sandwich potato salad	fiesta soup crackers peanut butter	beef pot pie apple chips	chicken noodle soup crackers peanut butter cups	h.m. pizza Fruit whip
PM Snack	marshmallow parfait	chocolate peanut butter dessert	Pudding cones	gelatin fruit bouquet	rocky road pudding	peachy-orange ring	self layering-dessert
Supper	tacos spanish rice mixed vegetables pineapple	chicken pot pie fruited tilt	pepper steak rice biscuits vegetables	hamburger gravy mashed potatoes fruit sorbet	sweet n sour chicken rice fruit	sloppy joes macaroni salad fruit	fajitas tortilla steak strips chips, salsa
Evening Snack	pudding cookies	apple cider dessert	fruited marble dessert	pudding pizza	jell-o jewel	boston crème pie	fruited chiffon-squares

Juli Brown

FOOD STORAGE
DAILY MENU RECORD

	Sunday	Monday	Tuesday	Wednesday	Thursday	Friday	Saturday
Breakfast	apple muffins juice	waffles milk	Cereal Milk Toast	pancakes fruit milk	banana muffins juice	cereal milk raisins	apple cobbler milk
Lunch	soft pretzel cheese jello jigglers	peanut butter crackers fruit	potato soup Bread Pumpkin pie	nachos beans salsa	pb & j bread pickles praline pie	tuna salad cornbread	fry bread beans cheese
PM Snack	quick apple pie	jello poke cake	under the sea Salad	creamy pumpkin desert	chocolate no bake oatmeal cookies	waldorf salad	jello trifle
Supper	vegetable soup fruit rolls	spaghetti sauce w/ meat vegetable garlic bread	ranch beans tortilla chips Fruit Cheese	beef and gravy potatoes fruit	chicken noodles vegetables bread	tostadas beans cheese fruit	bbq beef vegetable roll
Evening Snack	muddy buddies cookies	chocolate chip cookies	Russian tea Cakes	jello jigglers	sopapillas	chocolate pudding	jello popcorn

FOOD STORAGE
DAILY MENU RECORD

	Sunday	Monday	Tuesday	Wednesday	Thursday	Friday	Saturday
Breakfast	cheese	apple pancakes	bran muffin	cold cereal	oatmeal	toast	peach crepes
	toast	milk	milk	toast	raisins, cinnamon	applesauce	milk
	milk			milk	milk	milk	
Lunch	tuna salad	beefy tomato	chicken & stars	frito pie	veg beef soup	chicken salad	tomato soup
	in puff pastry	casserole,	soup	(ref beans, cheese,	bread	banana pudding	garden salad
		fruit	strawberry	onions, tomatoes,		crackers	cheese
			shortcake	lettuce, fritos)			sandwich
PM Snack	creamy apple	butterscotch bars	banana layered	pistachio pudding	chocolate turtle pie	bavarian crème	german sweet
	pecan pie		pie			pastry	chocolate pie
Supper	turkey & gravy	chili beans	chicken a la king	hamburger noodle	Chimichangas	bbq chicken	enchiladas
	mashed potatoes	tortillas	rice	casserole	Fruit	rice	tortilla chips
	cherry ice box	cheese	veg	fruit cups	cheese	veg	salsa
	cake		biscuits	biscuits			
	biscuits						
Evening Snack	brownies	stewed apples	oatmeal	fruit freeze	peanut butter	fruit salad	applesauce
			cookies		cookies		cake

109

Juli Brown

FOOD STORAGE
DAILY MENU RECORD

	Sunday	Monday	Tuesday	Wednesday	Thursday	Friday	Saturday
Breakfast	waffles syrup milk	cold cereal toast, jelly milk	french toast powdered sugar milk	cinnamon rolls Raisins Milk	oatmeal toast milk	cinnamon toast cereal milk	pancakes syrup milk
Lunch	grilled cheese sandwiches fruit slush	peanut butter jelly sandwich cinnamon apples	tuna sandwich chips pineapple snow	cheese toast bacon bits macaroni salad	pasta salad cornbread molasses crinkles	potato soup crackers cheese	peanut butter crackers, cheese frozen pumpkin squares
PM Snack	butterscotch bars	pound cake fruit	banana split pie	pudding ice cream	boston crème torte	lemon sundae pie	buried cookie dessert
Supper	beef stew rolls melon dessert	bean burros fruit spanish rice	chili cornbread fruit salad	chicken Rice Veg Rolls	nachos (beans, chips, cheese, onions, salsa) fruit salad	macaroni & cheese veg fruit tarts	vegie rice casserole (rice, beans carrots) layered coconut pecan rectangles
Evening Snack	chex mix	jello popcorn	empanadas	chocolate oatmeal Cookies	banana pudding vanilla wafers	peanut butter cookies	popcorn m&m's

FOOD STORAGE
DAILY MENU RECORD

	Sunday	Monday	Tuesday	Easter	Thanksgiving	Christmas	BBQ Holidays
Breakfast	cereal	french toast sticks	Peanut butter toast	pancakes	Cheese ball	oranges	cereal
	toast	syrup	Milk	milk	crackers	cinnamon rolls	toast
	milk	milk			oranges	milk	milk
Lunch	chicken salad	chicken & rice soup	Tuna sandwich	ham	Peanut butter	sub sandwiches	steak soup
	sandwich	crackers	Chips	potatoes	sandwiches	chips	cheese, crackers
	carrots	peanut butter	Applesauce	garden salad	Apple	fruit	
				rolls	carrot sticks	veg tray	
PM Snack	jello jigglers	banana frappe	Pudding pie	muddy buddies	veg appetizer tray	cheese balls	veg tray
				(recipe on the chex cereal box)		crackers	
Supper	hamburgers	pork chops	Roast	ham sandwiches	Turkey	tamales	hamburgers, hot dogs, potato salad, chips
	buns	rice	carrots, onions	cheese	mashed potatoes	enchiladas	pork & beans
	lettuce, tomatoes,cheese	veg	Potatoes	fruit tarts	gravy, stuffing,	tortilla chips	watermelon
	potato salad	rolls	Rolls		corn, rolls	salsa, spanish rice	
Evening Snack	pudding cups	fruited jello	ice cream	fresh fruit	Pie	pie	brownies

Juli Brown

FOOD STORAGE
DAILY MENU RECORD

	Day 1	Day 2	Day 3	Day 4	Day 5	Day 6	Day 7
Breakfast							
Lunch							
PM Snack							
Supper							
Evening Snack							

112

FOOD STORAGE
DAILY MENU RECORD

	Day 8	Day 9	Day 10	Day 11	Day 12	Day 13	Day 14
Breakfast							
Lunch							
PM Snack							
Supper							
Evening Snack							

Juli Brown

FOOD STORAGE
DAILY MENU RECORD

	Day 15	Day 16	Day 17	Day 18	Day 19	Day 20	Day 21
Breakfast							
Lunch							
PM Snack							
Supper							
Evening Snack							

114

FOOD STORAGE
DAILY MENU RECORD

	Day 22	Day 23	Day 24	Day 25	Day 26	Day 27	Day 28
Breakfast							
Lunch							
PM Snack							
Supper							
Evening Snack							

FOOD STORAGE
DAILY MENU RECORD

	Day 29	Day 30	Day 31	Easter	Thanksgiving	Christmas	BBQ Holidays
Breakfast							
Lunch							
PM Snack							
Supper							
Evening Snack							

About the Author

Juli has been teaching food storage classes for 20 years in her community to individuals, newlyweds and families. She also teaches home canning and food preservation. Juli tested her program by gathering her food storage and feeding her family from it for a year. Juli lives with her family in a small town near Phoenix Arizona.